Old Slamannan and Avonbridge
by John Hood

In this 1910 photograph sacks of grain are being loaded onto a horse-drawn cart outside Waugh's Avonbridge grain mill. Nearby, a second horse and cart are lined up ready for loading. The mill, which was established in the late 1800s, was located on the north bank of the River Avon on Blackston Road and was operated by Allan and James Waugh. In addition to the mill, a seed dressing plant was established to the rear of nearby Craigbank House. In 1937, after James's death, it was indicated that the firm would continue to carry on the business. Although initially the mill had ground wheat, barley and oats, in its final years it largely only mixed and blended grains brought into the mill from the company's main depot at Haymarket in Edinburgh. Notwithstanding, Waugh's maintained a local presence until the early 1970s, when the mill was demolished. Today, a small public park stands on its site. To the extreme right of the picture, a portion of Gardner's woollen mill can be seen.

© John Hood, 2015
First published in the United Kingdom, 2015,
by Stenlake Publishing Ltd.
www.stenlake.co.uk
ISBN 9781840337129

The publishers regret that they cannot supply
copies of any pictures featured in this book.

Acknowledgements

I would like to thank the following for their help: Geoff Bailey, Georgie Baird, Willie Dunsmore, Malvena Dwyer, Mary and Robert Inglis, Betty Mercer, Alan and Willie Fleming, Joyce Ligertwood, Margaret McGeever, Kiki Pason, John Robertson, and Billy and Catriona Stevenson. The publisher and author wish to thank Willie Fleming, Robert Inglis and Margaret McGeever for permission to reproduce the photographs on pages 1, 25, 33, 34, 39, 46 and 48

Further Reading

The books listed below were used by the author during his research. Those interested in finding out more are advised to contact their local studies library.

Hutton, Guthrie, *Mining from Kirkintilloch to Clackmannan & Stirling to Slamannan*, Stenlake Publishing, 2000.
Ligertwood, Joyce, *Annals of Avonbridge*, n.d.
Murray, Andrew, *Fifty Years of Slamannan Co-operative Society Limited 1861-1911*, Slamannan Co-operative Society Limited, 1911.
Slamannan Local History Group, *Slamannan and Limerigg: times to remember*, Falkirk Local History Society, 1990.
Thomson, Frank, *Pits, Pints and Poverty: an account of the village of Standburn*, Falkirk District Libraries, 1984.
Waugh, Rev. James, *Slamannan Parish through the Changing Years*, Falkirk District Council 1977.

The Lin Mill Falls, seen here around 1924, lie on the fast flowing Lin Mill Burn which rises at Wester Burnhead Farm, near Whitburn, and thereafter flows north before emptying into the River Avon near Newland Mill. Inevitably, the sixty feet high falls proved (despite parental disapproval) to be an irresistible attraction to generations of local Avonbridge children, who would come here to picnic and paddle or guddle for trout. Since this photograph was taken, the erection of new housing has somewhat restricted access to the falls. A further attraction in earlier times was the nearby Lin Mill meal mill, one of several in the vicinity. In October 1900, while tenanted by grain merchant James Waugh, the mill was offered for let: at that time, it utilised three pairs of stones driven by water and steam power. The mill finally ceased operation in the 1950s. Also nearby was Linhouse Farm, known locally as the 'Lennis', where scones and pancakes could be bought.

Introduction

The villages of Avonbridge, Limerigg, Slamannan and Standburn, known collectively as the Southern Braes villages, lie on the windswept Slamannan plateau which, near the Black Loch, reaches a height of almost 700 feet. While the soil near the River Avon (which is prone to flooding) is fertile, much of the upper areas comprise damp and infertile moorland. Historically therefore farming has always been problematic, which lends credibility to the reputed derivation of Slamannan as being a corruption of 'ploughing his land would slay man and mare' – a comment made by an early farmer to his feudal landlord. Notwithstanding, at one time the parish supported no less than thirty-nine farms. Of varying size, many, such as Craigend Farm, were part of a larger estate and often let on long leases. The harshness of the conditions on the plateau, however, meant that crops were harvested months later than those in the lower and more fertile lands. Associated with the farming industry were ancillary trades such as milling, construction, weaving, shoemaking and blacksmithing.

If land on the plateau wasn't particularly arable, it did have abundant deposits of good quality coal. For centuries numerous small pits, many originally operated as private concerns, were worked throughout Slamannan Parish: although here too, the land posed a problem, as water would seep through the peat just below the surface and often cause the collapse of mine workings. The exploitation of these coal seams was greatly expanded when, in 1840, the Slamannan Railway was opened, making it easier for mine owners to transport their coal to the markets in Glasgow and Edinburgh. Initially, the line ran between Airdrie and Manuel, but very soon thereafter a network of branch lines was opened to connect with some of the larger pits such as Jawcraigs, where at one time sixteen pits were worked. These pits had the added advantage of producing some of the best (and cheapest) coking coal on the market at that time, including the famed Balquhatstone Jewel and Virtuewell. As the industry expanded, small mining villages were established at Binniehill, Limerigg, Southfield and Standburn. Such was the growth of the industry that, by 1886, it was estimated that 2,000 men and boys were employed in the coal mines in the Slamannan area alone. This growth was reflected in the increase in population, which surged to a peak of over 7,000 in 1891. However, as coal seams became exhausted and many of the pits closed, the population decreased, dipping to a low of 3,443 in 1911. By 1921 only a small number of pits were still in operation, so much so that census figures produced in 1923 show that Slamannan Parish had suffered a decrease in population of 49.4% – caused primarily by miners leaving the area in search for work, but also by the attendant decline in associated industries such as quarrying, brick-making and milling. Particularly affected was the mining village of Standburn, where virtually the entire community was resettled in a new model village at nearby Westquarter in the mid-1930s.

Life on the plateau was particularly harsh during winter months, when it was quite common for roads and railway lines to be blocked for days on end by drifts of up to seven feet. In January 1936, for example, two buses proceeding in opposite directions between Falkirk and Slamannan became embedded in snowdrifts and had to be dug out. At the same time pupils from Slamannan and Avonbridge who were attending school in Falkirk had to remain there overnight. The next morning two special buses (one carrying men armed with shovels) and a police patrol car were laid on to bring the pupils home. Although this operation was successful, on the return journey both the buses and the police car were embedded in the snowdrifts, resulting in the police car being abandoned overnight!

A further problem for the inhabitants of the Southern Braes villages was their relative isolation, exacerbated by a lack of transport links. The introduction of passenger services in 1840 on the Slamannan Railway, with stations at Avonbridge, Blackston and Slamannan, had a huge impact on the social life of the inhabitants. However, passenger services in the area ceased in 1930. This, to an extent, was compensated for with the introduction of regular bus services such as those provided by Wilson Marshall of Standburn and Walter Alexander & Sons.

Notwithstanding improvements in housing and environmental works (such as sewage schemes), in 1943 a Regional Survey of Central and the South East of Scotland, set up to consider the restoration of de-populated areas and the reclamation of derelict land, found that it would be 'especially difficult' on the Slamannan plateau, which they described as being a 'derelict area of peat bog and old worn out mining sites with their bings and rush covered fields'. Over the years this forecast has proved to be accurate because, despite the best efforts of various government departments, the difficulties referred to previously have acted to discourage the introduction of new industry (with the exception of forestry) into the area. In recent years efforts have been made to reclaim derelict sites and remove unsightly industrial workings. Nowadays, many of the inhabitants of the Southern Braes villages are no longer employed locally and instead commute to towns in the Central Belt.

As late as the 1920s, when this photograph was taken, Brownrigg was an independent little community of less than a dozen houses, located just west of Slamannan. Since that time, however, it has been absorbed into Slamannan itself. Several of the properties seen here still survive, including the semi-detached property on the left, which at the time of writing comprises Woodside Cottage and Carridene. The taller property with roof dormers has been replaced, albeit with a building built in a similar style. The furthest away property, Balnagowan Cottage, is now much altered. Built around 1900, it originally comprised two houses but around fifty years ago was converted into one. Just out of picture, on the opposite side of the road from Balnagowan, are Brownrigg Cottage and the Sheiling, both of which were built before 1900.

A 1920s photograph of Slamannan Public School in Bank Street. The earliest portion of the school (which was built shortly after the formation of the Slamannan School Board) dates from 1875 and replaced an earlier building which was known locally as the 'Slate School'. The new school, seen here, was built at a cost of £2,500 and officially opened in September 1876. In 1932 the school building was 'reconstructed' at a cost of around £12,000 to give it eight classrooms, a large hall and changing rooms. At the same time the arched front porch and the central roof steeple (both seen here) were removed. In addition an extension to house Advanced Division scholars was built within the school grounds. This comprised four classrooms, together with cookery and technical rooms. The 'reconstruction' was carried out by the County Architect, Mr A.N. Malcolm, and officially opened in September 1932 by County Councillor George McLaren. In the early 1960s the extension burnt down but it was replaced in 1968.

In this 1929 photograph, looking down Bank Street, the stone wall at the entrance to the Old School House, adjacent to the school, is on the extreme left of the photograph. This house is now privately owned, but in years gone by provided accommodation for teachers at the school. The two-storey tenement building on the left is now gone, as is the one further along the street. On the right-hand side of the street, in the middle distance, is Bank House. Originally known as Balcastle Villa, this property was built in 1857 for coal master William Scott. It was later sold to James Nimmo (another coal master), who ultimately let it to the City of Glasgow Bank. Very shortly afterwards, in 1878, the bank collapsed, but almost immediately the property was taken over by the Bank of Scotland. In 1895 new bank premises were built adjoining Bank House and the house was converted to provide accommodation for the then bank manager, Thomas Mitchell, who continued to live in the house until his death in 1933. In early 1968 the bank relocated to new premises in the High Street and, later that same year, Bank House was demolished. Today, Castlehill Filling Station and Slamannan Health Clinic occupy the site of Bank House.

Further down Bank Street, almost at the beginning of High Street, was Binniehill House – undoubtedly the grandest of the 'big' houses in Bank Street. In this early 1900s view its lodge house and gate pillars can be seen on the right-hand side of the street. The house, which was set in four acres of ground, was built in 1857 for local coal master Dr Brown. It was later acquired, firstly, by James McKillop and then, in 1893, by James Liddell (both also coal masters). The latter resided in the house until his death in January 1920. Thereafter it was the residence of his widow, Jane, until her death in November 1925. Shortly before her death Binniehill House had been put up for sale for the upset price of £1,800. At that time it comprised three public rooms, eight bedrooms, kitchen, bathroom and laundry, a three-stalled stable, garage and two greenhouses. As no buyer could be found, it was offered for the reduced upset price of £1,000 and was ultimately bought for £1,465 for use as a Jewish Convalescent Home. Between 1933 and 1950 it was occupied by local newsagent Miss Elizabeth Downs. It was ultimately demolished in the 1970s.

This photograph, issued as a postcard around 1918 by local stationer John Irvine, was taken from the foot of Bank Street, looking west. The stone gate pillar on the left marks the entrance to Gowanlea House. From 1868 this was occupied by local doctor John Boyd until his death in 1902, and thereafter by his widow, Agnes, who died there in 1908. Although the original stone gate pillars and wrought iron gates still stand, Gowanlea House itself has now been divided into flats. Further up Bank Street, the second set of gate pillars seen here mark the entrance to Binniehill House. Of the three single-storey cottages on the right-hand side of the street, only two remain – the cottage on the extreme right now being the site of a memorial garden honouring local Victoria Cross holder Samuel Frickleton. The two-storey tenement in the far distance has also since been demolished. In the early 1900s this contained Mrs Affleck's 'jenny-a-things' shop. Other traders in Bank Street during the same period included Jennie Easton (bookseller, stationer and confectioner) and John Baxter (draper).

In this late 1920s photograph, looking east towards Slamannan Cross, all of the older properties on High Street can be seen. While those on the left-hand side of the street have survived largely unchanged, all of the properties on the right were demolished around 1960. When this photograph was taken, the four shops on the extreme left were occupied by Alexander Calder (grocer), Samuel Affleck (cobbler), William Wilkie (joiner) and George Smith (barber). Between 1950 and 1970 the grocery shop (extreme left of the photograph) was in the ownership of Lizzie Downs, who ran it as a newsagent and grocer. Around 2009 this shop traded as McClenaghan's Village Shop, selling newspapers, groceries and snacks, but at the time of writing is empty and boarded-up. Occupying a prominent position on the opposite side of High Street is the Waddell Clock Monument. It was sculpted by Joseph Hayes in the form of an obelisk and included a clock and two drinking fountains. It was erected in 1902 in memory of George Ralston Peddie Waddell of Balquhatstone, who was killed at Germiston during the Boer War. The monument was unveiled in front of a sizeable crowd in July of that year by George Ure of Wheatlands.

For over a century Slamannan Cross, seen here around 1914, was dominated by two popular hostelries – the St Lawrence Spirit Vaults and the Royal Hotel. The former (second building on the extreme left of the photograph) was established in 1864 and at that time was run by publican John Dickson. The public house was later run by the McAllister family, who allowed the use of one of the upper rooms for meetings of Thistle Lodge No. 32 Free Gardeners. On the opposite corner to the Spirit Vaults was the equally long-established Royal Hotel which, around the time this photograph was taken, was run by publican Thomas Smith. In 1877 the availability of drink from these and other local licensed premises led James McKillop of Binniehill House to support the work of the Women's Temperance Prayer Union, whose efforts were in fact particularly directed against licensed grocers. It was thought that these grocers were prone to encouraging housewives to disguise their secret drinking habits by entering alcohol sales in their pass books as 'aqua', 'soap', etc.! At the time of writing the Royal Hotel is in a poor state of repair, having lain derelict for a number of years.

In the early 1900s this junction of High Street and Pirnie Lodge (later Avonbridge) Road was known locally as the 'Ting Tong corner' due to the presence of a branch of the Ting Tong Tea Company on the corner (just out of picture to the extreme right). After the demise of the branch and the opening nearby of an evangelical mission, it then became known as the 'Sunshine Corner'. The square pillars built into the stone wall on the left mark the entrance to the United Free Church Manse, while further down in the middle distance is the entrance to New Street. On the right-hand side of the road, in Smithy Field, is Charles McLean's smiddy. This was established around 1824 by McLean's father-in-law, Robert Taylor. By all accounts Taylor was very much respected locally and on several occasions was presented with a purse of gold sovereigns by grateful citizens. In 1903 the smiddy was taken over by Angus McLean, who had the distinction of being the last working blacksmith in the Slamannan Parish.

By 1929, when this photograph was taken, Smithy Field had been utterly transformed, firstly by the building of a striking war memorial and, secondly, by the construction of a miners' welfare hall. The former occupies a prominent corner site and comprises a marble obelisk with three flanking red granite lion statues. In memory of the fifty-two men of Slamannan, Limerigg and district who lost their lives in the Great War, it was unveiled on 15 October by Mrs Mitchell, the wife of the local Bank of Scotland branch manager, in the presence of 300 spectators. After the unveiling, an address was given by Major R. Glyn, MP for Clackmannanshire and East Stirlingshire, and a volley of shots was fired by a detachment of the 7th Argyll and Sutherland Highlanders. To the rear of the war memorial is the Slamannan Miners' Welfare Institute. Its construction was partly funded by a grant of £38,000 disbursed by the Lanarkshire Miners' Welfare Committee and it was fitted out with baths, billiard tables, carpet bowls, library, offices and a kitchen. It was officially opened in September 1925 by Thomas Bell, the Commercial Manager of nearby Jawcraigs Colliery. In 1950 the institute was put up for sale and later renovated for use as private housing.

Main Street, Slamannan — Valentines Series

In this view from around 1905 many of the properties that lined Main Street from the Cross to Bridgend can be clearly seen. At the Cross itself are the St Lawrence Spirit Vaults on the extreme left of the photograph and the Royal Hotel on the extreme right. Until comparatively recent times, both sides of Main Street were lined with a wide variety of well-patronised shops such as John Irvine's ironmonger. The most significant of the local traders, however, was the Slamannan Co-operative Society Limited, which commenced business here on 7 June 1861. The society, which arose from a meeting of co-operatively-minded local colliers, initially leased a house on Yankee's Land on Main Street. However, within six years it had erected a purpose-built store on Main Street for the sale of groceries and footwear. This store, and later extensions, was contained within the row of single-storey buildings seen here in the middle distance beside the horse and cart. The redevelopment of Main Street in the early 1960s resulted in the demolition of many of the older properties seen here.

This 1911 view shows the extensive frontage of the Slamannan Co-operative Society store on Main Street. The original store had occupied approximately two-thirds of the building seen here and sold only groceries and footwear. However, in 1887 an extension was added for the sale of drapery goods. Subsequent extensions included offices, a dressmaking workshop and a tailor's cutting room to the rear of the property, and a tailor's workshop above the drapery department, with all the clothes made being sold within the premises. Also on Main Street, in a separate property, was a bakehouse. Earlier, in 1873, a second store had been opened on Station Road, which also sold groceries. This property had been bought from local coal master, John Watson, and comprised a store with attached dwelling houses. Later, in 1893, the bakehouse on Main Street was replaced with a much larger and more modern bakery to the rear of the Station Road store. Further expansion followed in Avonbridge and Limerigg, and continued until 1958 when a series of closures began, including that of the Station Road store in 1965. In 1966 the Slamannan Co-operative Society Limited was finally absorbed into Falkirk and District United Co-operative Society.

The Children's Gala held on Saturday 7 June 1911, to mark the fiftieth anniversary of the Slamannan Co-operative Society Limited, was celebrated in great style despite the inclement weather. In total, some 1,400 children from Slamannan and the surrounding villages took part in a parade. The children from Slamannan and Limerigg assembled on the Limerigg Road at Burn Row, whilst those coming from further afield were brought into Slamannan Station by a special train. At the station the children were grouped by locality and marched by way of New Street, Main Street and Bank Street to Blinkbonnie. In this view, the parade is seen passing William Fraser's Royal Hotel at the junction of Main Street and High Street. To commemorate the event, Main Street (and the Society's premises) was decorated with streamers of evergreen, the street lamps were adorned with rhododendron blossoms, and bannerettes were put up. At Blinkbonnie the parade temporarily dispersed, with the participants congregating in a field belonging to Castlehill Farm, where juice and buns were handed out. Afterwards the children took part in a programme of sports before reassembling and retracing their steps until they reached Mosscastle Road.

In this 1909 view, looking towards Slamannan Cross and High Street, some of the older properties on Main Street can be seen. On the extreme left is Robert Hamilton's butcher shop (which by the 1920s was occupied by butcher Alexander Brodie). Next to Hamilton's shop, and just out of picture, was a two-storey building occupied by Peter Grant (saddler) and George Dobbie (fruiterer). The single-storey building beyond the cart is Slamannan Co-operative Society's store, followed by the Royal Hotel. Shops which were located on the right-hand side of the street included Nimmo (newsagent), Alexander Gillespie (plumber), and Alexander Bennie (butcher). Directly facing the camera, at the Cross, are the shops belonging to Robert Wilson and Henry Rennie (both of whom were licensed grocers). To the rear of these High Street shops, we can just get a glimpse of the roof and spire of the old Slamannan Free Church. Although many of the buildings to the left of the photograph have survived, the majority of those from the extreme right up to and including the two-storey property in middle distance have been demolished and replaced with new housing.

In this view of Slamannan Cross from around 1929, the main activity seems to be centred outside the Royal Hotel and the St Lawrence Spirit Vaults. Perhaps the men were waiting for opening time! At one time the St Lawrence Spirit Vaults were owned by John Dickson and in 1860 he also acquired the local gas works on the death of the owner, James Wilson (also a local grocer). For the next eight years John Dickson's gas works supplied Slamannan's gas until they were sold to the Slamannan Gaslight Company Ltd in 1868. To the right of the Clock Monument is a branch of the ACME Dairy Company. This was owned by John Baird of Falkirk, the company having several shops throughout Central Scotland, including their main branch, offices and storerooms in Grahams Road, Falkirk. Also in view is a single-deck omnibus operated by Wilson Marshall & Sons' Venture Bus Company. Until their acquisition by the Scottish Motor Traction Company (SMT) in March 1930, Marshall's provided a daily passenger service between Falkirk and Slamannan.

In this early 1900s' view of Main Street at Bridgend, the 'Slate School' and Bridgend Inn (two of Slamannan's best known properties) can be seen. The former, on the extreme left, was a two storey rubble-built property with matching skeyputs, erected in 1776. It was originally known as the Slate House but in 1804, when premises were needed to house Slamannan's first school, it was decided that the ground floor would be converted for use as classrooms while the upper floor would become living accommodation for the schoolmaster. An external stair was also added in order to give the schoolmaster access to his premises. In this view some of the pupils can be seen in the doorway of the school. The building later served as a hall for the local Orange Order and, ultimately, a hardware shop run by Robert McAlpine. It was finally demolished in the 1960s. The open area between the school and the single-storey white-washed Bridgend Inn was later filled by the Slamannan Masonic Hall. Just beyond the roof of the inn can be seen the twin roof dormers of Ladysland. Dating from around 1890, this house still survives despite the extensive road realignment nearby. On higher ground beyond Ladysland is Slamannan Parish Church.

Almost all of the properties seen here at Bridgend have now gone, including the house on the right and the Masonic Hall of Lodge St John No. 484, second on the left. This lodge was established in 1868 and initially met in the Royal Hotel, and later in the Crown Inn. The foundation stone of the new hall was laid on 17 August 1901 by George Christie, the Provincial Grand Master of Stirlingshire, using a solid silver trowel presented by the architect and contractors. Despite inclement weather, the occasion was a grand affair with no less than three bands joining the procession of invited guests. Along the route the parade was joined by the Thistle Lodge No. 32 Free Gardeners, headed by the Blackbraes Brass Band. The building was designed by Falkirk architect William Black and construction cost approximately £1,300. On the ground floor there were three dwelling houses, each comprising two rooms and a kitchen. The hall itself was on the upper floor, together with two ante-rooms, a cloakroom and a toilet. In later years, the hall was used for weddings and bingo sessions, but was demolished when Main Street was realigned.

In this photograph from 1929 all the principal buildings of Slamannan Parish Church can be seen on both sides of the Falkirk road at the top of the village. These include the church hall, the manse and the parish church. The first, on the left, was built in 1846 and is largely unchanged, although a modern brick-built extension has been added. Comprising a main hall (with stage), rear room, kitchen, toilets and store rooms, the building is at the time of writing lying empty and up for sale. The manse, set further back beyond the trees, was built in 1857 for the Rev. Robert Horne, one of Slamannan's most illustrious ministers. It replaced a much earlier building which reputedly had been 'frequently repaired and extended'. In 1985 the manse seen here burnt down and in 1989 was replaced by the present-day manse in Manse Place. At the time of writing this too is up for sale. To the rear of the 1857 manse was the 'glebe', which was used, amongst other things, for gala days and for Slamannan & District Agricultural Society annual shows.

THE AVON, SLAMANNAN.

On its journey through the parishes of Slamannan and Muiravonside, the River Avon bisects the main highway between Slamannan and Falkirk, just to the north of Slamannan. As such, the need for a bridge was important, not least to the local economy. The bridge shown in the photograph from around 1915 was known locally as the 'iron bridge' and was constructed in the 1880s. It was a single-span metal construction, supported by twin stone pillars. Built into its western face was a carved stone displaying a coat of arms of the Livingstone family (a local landowning family), and the date 1640, commemorating an earlier bridge which stood on the site. Although it had initially been adequate to meet demands, by the 1930s the bridge's lack of width meant that a replacement was required and in 1937 Stirling County Council invited interested parties to tender for the construction of a new bridge, to be built alongside the older structure. Later that year, the new bridge (on the B803) was formally opened and still stands today.

With the propensity of the nearby Culloch Burn (which runs behind the houses to the right of the photograph) to flood following heavy rain or sudden thaws, perhaps the laying out of New Street had not been the best of ideas! This view was supported by the Rev. Alexander Cameron who for many years represented Slamannan on the local council, and who opined in 1951 that when the burn flooded it entered 'the many old houses foolishly built on its bank'. In September 1930, for example, the *Scotsman* reported that, 'following twelve hours of torrential rain the residents of the street reportedly awoke to find it transformed into a rivulet, with water eddying and swirling at their doors.' All of the properties in this photograph from around 1905 have long since gone, with the exception of the Wesleyan Methodist Chapel (a part of its pitched tiled roof vestibule can be seen just beyond the group of people on the right-hand side of the street). The chapel, which was officially opened in March 1874, was sold to the Church of Christ in March 1917 for £100. It functioned as such from its formal opening in July of that year until 19 June 2005, when the last service was held. At the time of writing the chapel is being converted into a private house. Within the two-storey property to the right of the chapel was James Murphy's grocers. In addition to this shop, Murphy also operated a carriage hire and undertaker business – possibly owning the carriage shown here.

Perhaps the most spectacular feature of the Culloch Burn, which rises in the vicinity of Binniehill and then runs approximately north-east to join the River Avon at the 'glebe' in Slamannan, are the Rumlie Falls. In common with the Linmill Falls outside Avonbridge, these attracted generations of village children who would come here to picnic or guddle for burn trout. However, unlike the Linmill Falls, the pools here were much deeper and lined with timber from old mine workings, making them more dangerous. It was therefore not unusual for children to be seen off with the cry 'don't go near the Rumlie' ringing in their ears! Although the burn looks picturesque and fairly serene at this point, it was capable of wreaking havoc further downstream.

On Sunday, 4 August 1861, the congregation of Slamannan Free Church met to celebrate the formal opening of their new building. In a gesture of fellowship, the parish church minister, the Rev. R.S. Horne, suspended his church services for the day to enable his congregation to join in the celebrations. Sadly, in March 1864, as the congregation gathered for Sunday service, the church was badly damaged by fire. Fortunately, most of the contents of the building, including the seats, were saved and the rebuilt church (shown here) reopened shortly afterwards. In 1900 there was a change of name to the Slamannan United Free Church and it later became the Church of Scotland Slamannan Balquhatstone. In October 1945, following several previous unsuccessful attempts, the congregation reunited with the parish church to form Slamannan Parish Church. Finally, in May 1961 the church was taken over by Stirling County Council and subsequently demolished.

In the foreground, on either side of this 1902 photograph, can be seen the parapets of the bridge over the Culloch Burn. In addition, laid out in readiness along Station Road, are new water pipes, which Messrs Warren & Stewart of Glasgow commenced laying that year.

Right: In October 1893 work commenced on the construction of a bowling green on Station Road, alongside Slamannan United Free Church. The site, which was eight feet above the level of Station Road, was gifted by the Peddie Waddells of nearby Balquhatstone House. By May of the following year the green was ready for use and it was officially opened in June 1894 by James McKillop MP. The bowling green's first clubhouse, which can be seen here on the north side of the green, was built on ground gifted by local coal master James Liddell of Binniehill, and was officially opened in April 1935 by John Baxter. This served until the opening of a new clubhouse in May 1981 by J. Dick Peddie of Balquhatstone.

In 1840 a station was opened by the Slamannan Railway Company to the south of Slamannan on Binniehill (later Station) Road. In this early photograph the signal box and the level crossing gates can be seen. After closure in 1949 the line was lifted and the station buildings demolished, with the exception of the station master's cottage situated further down Station Road. This single-storey cottage with twin roof dormers is now divided into two homes – Almar and Station House. Although the substantial two-storey villa seen here in the centre of the picture has now gone, the cottage beyond Station House remains (now divided into two homes – North Most Cottage and South Most Cottage), as does Balquhatstone Cottage (seen here on the road bend, facing camera). Also remaining, but just out of picture on the right, is Bir Hakim, once the home and surgery of long-serving Slamannan doctor John Arthur. Adjacent to Bir Hakim once stood the store and bakery of Slamannan Co-operative Society. The store was a typical society building, comprising a shop with storage facilities above, and a single-storey extension which served as living accommodation for the salesman.

Slamannan Railway Station, looking east towards Avonbridge. This building housed the waiting room, parcel office and station master's office. Further along the track are the level crossing gates on Station Road and the signal box. Although it was mostly a single track railway system, at Slamannan there was a double track controlled by points which allowed trains to pass each other. Because of its proximity to the many local collieries and farms, the station was well patronised. In addition to normal traffic, it was also used for a variety of other activities. In 1909, for example, coal master James Nimmo conducted a sale of colliery plant and branch railway stock here. Similarly, in 1910 it is recorded that some 20,000 Ballachulish slates from Binniehill Farm were stacked at Slamannan Station waiting to be sold to any interested party.

This photograph was published as a postcard with the caption 'Pirnie Lodge Road' and Pirnie Lodge Farm lies approximately one mile east of Slamannan on the B8022. Built in 1735 for William Hastie and his wife Isabella, the farmhouse was greatly extended in 1867 when a single-storey extension was built onto the original house. Following the Disruption of 1843, when the majority of the congregation of the Slamannan Established Church left to join the Free Church of Scotland, the Hastie family (who were amongst those who left) offered the dissenters a site for their church on their land. Although the site was isolated, the offer was accepted and the new church opened in 1844. In 1977 one local historian recalled being told that the lack of a vestry in the church meant families presenting their child for baptism were obliged to wait with the Robertson family at nearby Crossburn Cottage until the minister was ready to start the ceremony! In spite of such drawbacks, the church served the congregation well. However, in 1860 a new site in Station Road, Slamannan, was gifted by Mrs Waddell of Balquhastone, and a new church opened in 1861. Pirnie Lodge farmhouse was later converted into an equestrian centre and, at time of writing, was for sale.

Prior to the opening of a local co-operative store, the inhabitants of the mining village of Limerigg acquired most of their groceries from a 'truck' shop operated by Nimmo & Burns, the owners of nearby Limerigg Colliery. However, in 1881, following a petition from Limerigg members of the Slamannan Co-operative Society, a branch store was opened to serve the village. The store, seen here in 1911, was a single-storey brick-built property containing both grocery and boot departments, with a dwelling house attached. In 1890 three double-dwelling houses were erected alongside, one of which is to the extreme right of the picture. During its lifetime, the store was generally successful, but as with any business it had its share of problems. In 1933, for example, it suffered a break-in when a number of articles were stolen, including a large quantity of tobacco, jars of malted food, cod liver oil emulsion, and 400 razor blades! In 1964, shortly before Slamannan Co-operative Society was taken over by nearby Falkirk & District United Co-operative Society, the Limerigg branch was closed.

For many years Ochilview House on Lochside Road was occupied by the Garlick family. The house comprised both family accommodation and a licensed grocers, which was run by the Garlicks (who also ran the post office, which adjoined the house). Until his death in January 1920, both businesses were run by Hiram Watson Garlick, who also represented Limerigg Parish Council on Stirling County Council for many years. After his death, the grocery business was briefly continued by son David, while the post office was run by local draper Alexander Hunter. In September 1923, Ochilview House (then occupied by Mrs Elizabeth Garlick), together with shop and stable, was offered up for sale or let. Also included in the sale were four adjoining single-storey houses. Around 1930 the licensed grocery shop was being run by J. Reynolds. Other than the post office (which has been demolished), all of the other buildings alongside Ochilview House, including West Ochilview Cottage, still stand today. Posing in front of the cottage in this photograph are May Grant and Margaret, Kate, Jean and Polly Rintoul.

Avonbridge, seen here from the south, was at one time an important crossing point on the River Avon, much used by drovers taking their cattle to the market in Falkirk. Initially, the greater part of the village was located on the north bank of the River Avon but gradually the open fields seen here to the south of Avonbridge United Reformed Church became occupied by new council housing which was erected in the 1930s and 1950s. In this early view, apart from what was then new housing built on the Slamannan Road, the area bordering Main Street (to the south of the church) remains as open fields. These fields, formerly part of the estate of Avonhill, were farmed by Robert Inglis of Lin Mill, who had gifted the land on which the church was built. In the far distance, to the left of the Falkirk road at the foot of Whinny Braes, is the row of seven white-washed single-storey buildings known locally as the 'White Raw'. The road to Lin Mill runs across the foreground of the photograph.

In this similar but closer view, taken slightly further to the west of the previous photograph, Avonbridge is again seen from the south. On this occasion, beyond Avonbridge United Reformed Church and manse (to the extreme right, mid-view) and Marshallfield Cottage (on the opposite side of the road), we can see a section of Main Street at the south end of Avonbridge. The road running between the stone walls in the foreground is the road to Lin Mill. To the extreme left, mid-view is the Headmaster's House and, alongside it, Avonbridge Combination School (both situated on the Slamannan Road). This school was a joint venture of the Muiravonside and Slamannan School boards and, when first erected, comprised a stone-built single-storey building with seven classrooms, but with no assembly hall or gymnasium. It also lacked a dining hall, so pupils had to eat their lunches at their desks. Access to the school was from two doors which could be used by both sexes. The school was later demolished and replaced, approximately on the same site, with the new Avonbridge Primary School which opened in 1962.

Notwithstanding the difficulties of the terrain and the relative infertility of the soil, Slamannan Parish once supported no less than thirty-nine farms. Although many have now gone, Craigend Farm, seen here, has survived. Situated on the Slamannan Road to the west of Avonbridge, this was originally the home farm for James Paton's nearby Avonhill Estate. The farmhouse itself was built in 1829 by local contractor Robert Thom and externally is largely unchanged. Among the occupants who have farmed here are Thomas Crawford and John Binnie. In 1926, while in the hands of Robert Binnie, the farm was put up for sale. He was then followed by James Johnston, who farmed at Craigend for about forty-five years until his retirement in 1969. Since then the farm has been run by several generations of the Inglis family. During their time the farm has supported a herd of approximately sixty Friesian cows, whose milk was originally collected by the Milk Marketing Board and currently by Wiseman's Dairies.

In February 1872, following the sequestration of Fraserburgh merchant Charles McBeath, the thirty-five-acre Avonhill Estate near Avonbridge was offered for sale within the Golden Lion Hotel, Stirling, for the upset price of £800. Its purchaser was James Paton, a partner in the Edinburgh publishing firm of Messrs Hugh Paton & Sons, whose main residence was in Corstorphine, Edinburgh. Until his death around 1910, Avonhill House was maintained by Paton as a country retreat. While resident there, he took a keen interest in local affairs and was elected onto the first Slamannan School Board in 1873. In this photograph, taken in 1908, Paton is seen with members of the congregations of the two local Avonbridge churches, prior to their visit that year to the Scottish National Exhibition held on the Saughton Hall Estate outside Edinburgh. The exhibition, which opened on 1 May, featured among its many attractions a water chute said to be the largest in the 'kingdom', a giant helter skelter and a figure of eight railway.

The tiny hamlet of Hillhead lies on the road to Westfield (B8047) just to the east of the Lin Mill Burn, which formerly marked the boundary between the parishes of Avonbridge and Muiravonside. In the foreground, the stone parapets of the bridge over the burn can be seen. Despite being within Muiravonside Parish, the children in the hamlet were permitted to attend Avonbridge Combination School. As the distance involved meant that the children couldn't go home for lunch, most of them carried a sandwich and a tin tea flask (in the 1920s and 1930s many of them would have purchased their lunch from Graham Forrester's general store on Main Street, Avonbridge). Since this photograph was taken, the first two cottages on the left nearest the camera have gone, although the building next to them still stands and appears largely unchanged externally. The latter, although officially known as the Hillhead Cottages, was known locally as the 'Sparra Row'. At one time this property was owned by Johnny Lennox, a popular local Sunday school teacher and Rechabite, who, amongst other things, organised the popular Sunday school trips. The fourth, and furthest away, property (which was a working smiddy until the 1970s) is still standing. Also remaining is the two-storey building, which is opposite the old smiddy and stands at the junction of the Westfield and Armadale roads. Originally known as Hillhead, this property is now called Linmill Cottage.

Linhouse, seen here around 1905, was for many years the country home of the Edinburgh lawyer and Clerk to the Signet James Home. In November 1836 the lands, barony and estate of Linhouse, together with his house in George Square, Edinburgh, were offered up for judicial sale to be sold by public roup on Wednesday, 23 November. Later, in 1848, all of the household goods were offered up for sale with buyers advised that 'ready money and discount allowed'. Notwithstanding the proposed sale, the house remained in the family's hands until the early 1900s. Clearly the sender of this postcard was living rough as in their message they commented, 'we are picnicking minus any servants, it is tremendous fun and glorious weather'.

In this view of Main Street, Avonbridge, looking north and taken around 1907, a pony and trap has just passed the United Reformed Church and manse (on the extreme right) and Marshallfield Cottage (on the opposite side of the road), heading for the Westfield road. To the left of Marshallfield Cottage, the open fields are now occupied by the new Avonbridge Primary School. Also visible (to the left of the trees in the middle of the photograph) is Alberdt Buildings, with its distinctive twin roof dormers. This property, situated at the junction of Slamannan Road and Main Street, was named after Mary Alberdt, whose post office, drapery and grocery store occupied part of the ground floor of the building in the early 1900s. In the distance, to the north of the railway station and on the left side of the photograph, is the distinctive form of the Avonbridge Parish Church with its bellcote and high-pitched tiled roof.

The Avonbridge United Reformed Church, known locally as the 'middle' church, was established in 1844 by the Rev. James Morrison as an Evangelical Union congregation. Today, it is largely unchanged externally and still retains the distinctive little bellcote above the front door. However, the open fields around it have long since been filled with housing. Just in picture, on the extreme right, is the former church manse which was built with monies gifted by local farmer Robert Inglis of Craigend Farm. At the time of writing the manse is derelict and boarded-up, but the church is still in use. Hidden from view, but situated between the manse and church, is the single-storey church hall. To the left of the picture, and partially screened by trees, is Marshallfield Cottage. This predates the church and for a long time was the home of the Gilchrist family. In 1913 the cottage was occupied by John Gilchrist, a local joiner and builder, who died there in the March of that year.

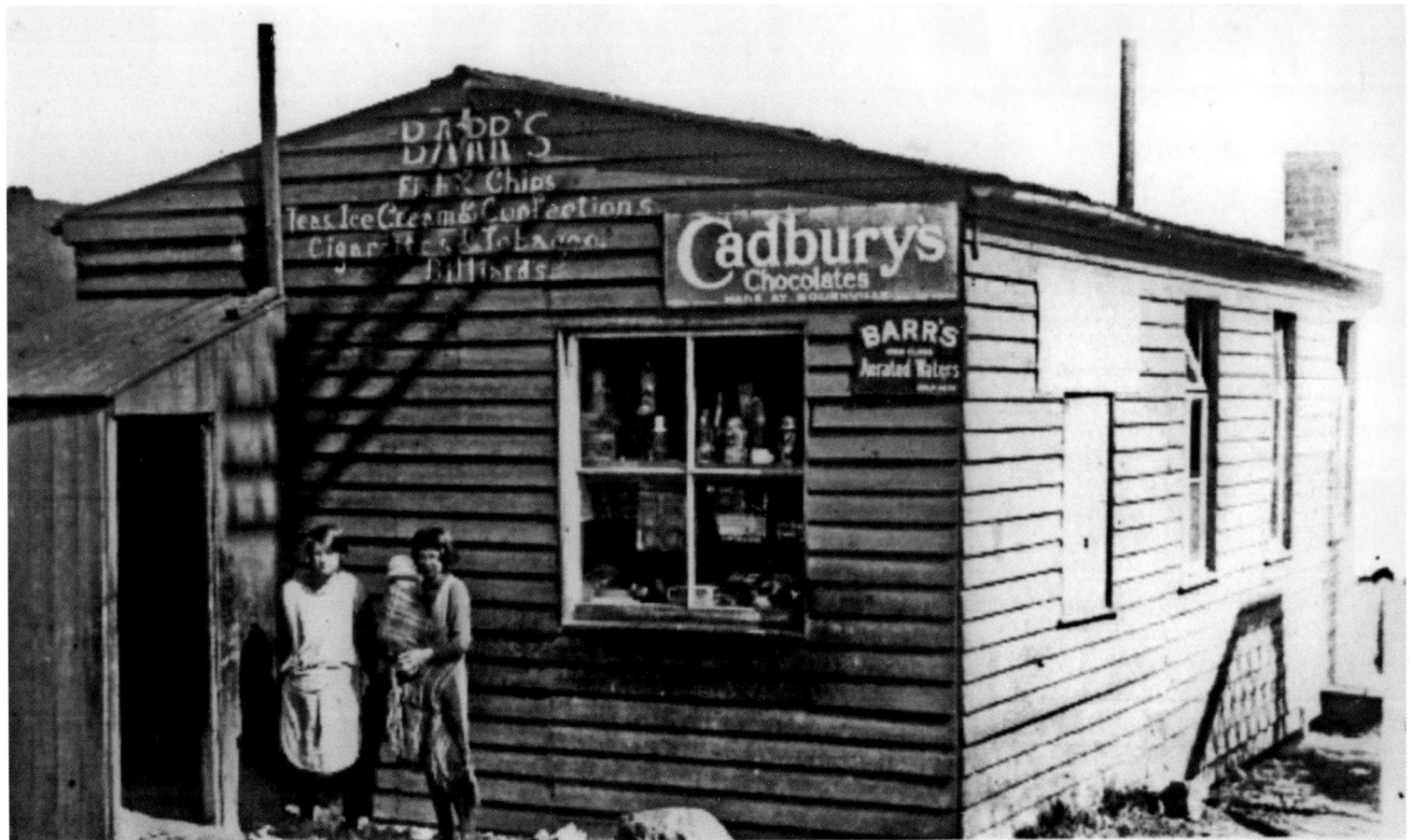

One of the most recognisable shops in Avonbridge was Jessie Barr's wooden shop on Main Street. Seen here around 1930, it was in many ways a 'jenny-a-things'. Jessie sold groceries such as sugar and rice (both stored in barrels), and butter and cheese (kept in tubs). In addition she also sold confectionery, tobacco, ice cream, and fish and chip suppers. During and after the Second World War, when rationing was in force, a particular favourite with local children were penny caramels, although a half-penny worth of chocolate chews was also popular! In retirement, Jessie continued to sell some items of confectionery from the hallway of her house at Craigbank. Meantime, the wooden shop was converted into a fish and chip shop, complete with small tearoom, run by local man, Adam McNaughton. In 1961 it was taken over by Slamannan Co-operative Society, who subsequently demolished the shop and built a new co-operative store on the site. The new store was officially opened in February 1965 by the society's Managing Secretary, William Bennie, and the original co-operative store at Bridgehillend was closed.

In this early view looking north, some of the older properties on Main Street, just to the south of its junction with Slamannan Road, can be seen. Among the properties to left of the photograph is a two-storey tenement known locally as Forrester's Building. This building, which has survived the almost wholesale demolition of Main Street, was named after the long-established local merchant Robert Forrester who was in business between 1893 and 1921. In addition to running the local post office, Robert sold groceries, clothes and newspapers. By 1921 the business (minus the post office) was run by Graham Forrester. Today, a doctor's surgery occupies part of the property. The detached building with the single roof dormer alongside Forrester's Building, has also survived, and presently houses the post office and village store. The property with the twin roof dormers on the opposite side of the street, on the right of the photograph, is Rosebank. For many years this was the family home of flax, seed and manure merchant Allan Waugh, whose lorries were garaged to the rear of the property. The waste ground in the right foreground is today occupied by a police station.

In this 1920s photograph, taken on Main Street just short of the junction with Slamannan Road, the most prominent building is the Alberdt Buildings, on the left, with its twin roof dormers. When this photograph was taken, the post office and shop, which were situated on the ground floor, were run by Charles Thorburn Marshall and continued to be until his death in February 1929. In 1936 the Alberdt Buildings, which comprised a shop and three houses, were put up for sale by the then owner, who, incidentally, was also selling at the same time a tenement of twelve houses in nearby Westfield. In the late 1950s the shop (minus post office) was run by Ignacy Jakubowski. At that time, a door to the rear of the shop led to his living room and kitchen, with three bedrooms upstairs. The other houses in the property were at that time occupied by Sanny Allan. Sanny was a local merchant who, in addition to his coal and undertakers businesses, dispensed petrol from the two pumps outside his house. For many years, the grassy area opposite the Alberdt Buildings was used as a fairground in the period around Gala Day. Today, this area has been landscaped and the village war memorial has been sited prominently on the corner. Alongside this is now the single-storey post office and village store.

This further view of Main Street, taken around 1908, offers a closer view of the older properties seen in the previous photograph. To the left is the row of single-storey cottages which were, variously, occupied by Jessie Chalmers' sweetie shop and butchers Robert Hamilton and John Waddell, who occupied separate shops which had a shared entrance. Like many butcher shops of the period, they had sawdust-covered floors and carcasses hung on hooks awaiting cleaving. Also in business here was Willie Hendry, who charged batteries, and 'Joe the barber', who had previously been a postman in Bathgate. The two-storey property beyond the row of cottages is Penman's Buildings. This, like the cottages, is long since gone. Also demolished is the building with the distinctive roof dormers, to right of picture. In the early 1900s a smiddy operated by John Hill was situated to the rear of this property, where horses were shoed and farm equipment repaired. In middle distance, the low stone wall to the right of the horse and cart marks the parapet of the bridge that carries Main Street (or Bridge Street, as it was then) over the River Avon.

In this early view of Avonbridge looking east, many of the properties on the north bank of the River Avon can be seen. Among them, on the extreme left, are the railway station buildings, including ticket office, footbridge and signal box. Immediately to the right of the footbridge is Bogo View, which at one time housed the village bakery and post office. Next to this are the properties at Binniehill, which included the Bridgehill Inn and Mary Bryce's sweetie shop. Also in view is Waugh's meal mill and, to the extreme right, Messrs A. & D. Gardner's woollen mill. The last-named was known locally as the 'blanket factory'. In the foreground, on the north bank of the River Avon, is the local football ground which, because of the low-lying nature of the land, was subject to frequent flooding. Also affected by flooding were the fields surrounding the village and the properties on Main Street itself.

At various points on the River Avon and its several tributaries, water was drawn by means of lades, controlled by rudimentary sluice gates, to feed the several local meal and woollen mills. The lade seen here, for example, led into Alexander & David Gardner's Avonbridge Woollen Mill. This had been established in 1800 to manufacture a range of woven items including tweeds, bedcovers, plaidings, sheetings, flannels, druggets (rugs) and crumcloths – the latter being cloth that was laid under dining room tables to keep the floor or carpet clean. In October 1912, following the deaths of the original partners, the mill was advertised for sale by public roup at the upset price of £600. At that time the mill was advertised as comprising an engine boiler, five power looms, one hand loom, carding and spinning machinery, teasing and dyeing appliances, and with a good and plentiful water supply. Also for sale were the manager's house and office, a semi-detached villa, and the tenement known as Gardner's Building, the latter comprising six dwelling houses and shops. For a period later, the mill was used as a base by local haulage contractor, Willie Grant, but eventually, in the second half of the last century, it was demolished.

In this early view, the Avonbridge war memorial can be seen on its original site on high ground above the River Avon, alongside the Blackston Road. Unveiled on 24 October 1920 by local mining contractor Robert Forrester, it was dedicated by the Rev. James Garvie of Avonbridge United Free Church. In 1964 the memorial was moved to its present site in the middle of the village, at the junction of Main Street and Slamannan Road. Further down Blackston Road, beyond McGregor's Buildings, and to the right of the photograph, is Avonbridge Welfare Hall with its single-storey front porch. Built in the early 1920s, this hall has been the venue for countless village concerts, dances, picture shows and other community events. In the middle of the photograph, partially obscured by the tall trees at the river's edge, is the Avonbridge grain mill. Immediately beyond the mill is the stone-arched bridge which carries Main Street across the River Avon. When Main Street was realigned in the 1970s, this bridge was widened and one side now has a concrete facade and the other a stone facade.

In this early 1900s view delivery man Willie Fleming is seen on the Slamannan Road, outside the East Lodge gate of Avonhill House. The horse and cart was one of several used by local grain merchants Allan and James Waugh to deliver oats, pigeon food and hen meal around the district. The supply of hen meal was particularly important as the area supported several large poultry farms. Typical of these was Balcastle Poultry Farm, run initially by Thomas Miller and then by his daughters, the Misses Millers. Throughout the 1920s this poultry farm was particularly active in selling large numbers of WB, Exchequer Leghorn, and Rhode Island Red chicks within and outwith the district. Some years after the death of Jessie Miller, Balcastle Poultry Farm was put up for sale. Included in the sale, in addition to Balcastle House, a steading, garage, coach house, harness room, byre and stable, were two Miller's Peerless Poultry Houses and one Miller's Hatching House.

In this early view looking south-west, all of Avonbridge south of the railway line can be seen. The one exception is Alexandra Cottage (seen here on the extreme right of the photograph) which lies to the north of the track. For many years this was the home of cobbler-cum-stationmaster David Mitchell. The long line of freight wagons at the station testifies to its original purpose, which was to carry coal from the Slamannan coalfields. Later, a rudimentary passenger service was initiated, but by early 1930 the LNER were reporting that 'for some time past few people have been availing themselves of the trains which have been running practically empty entailing serious financial loss'. Consequently, passenger services were withdrawn on 1 May 1930 and parcels, and fresh fish, fruit, milk and meat, were collected from Bathgate by motor vehicles. However, freight services continued until the closure of the railway in 1964. Over the years the railway played a varied role in village life. For example, in March 1904 Donald Smeaton, the Liberal candidate for Stirlingshire, was met at the station by the Avonbridge Pipe Band and conducted to his meeting place in the village to the strains of highland music.

In 1891, following the death of the then publican, Alexander Dobbie, the long-established Bridgehill Inn was put up for sale. At that time it comprised a kitchen, three rooms, bar and pantry on the ground floor, and one large room and two smaller rooms on the upper floor. Also included in the sale were cellarage (described as 'excellent'), stable, coach house and other offices, plus an adjoining two-storey dwelling house. It was subsequently acquired by publican John Ponton, who ran it until his retirement in 1906. In 1908, shortly after Ponton's death, his widow, Isabella, organised an important sale of bonded malt and grain whiskies, brandies, old-blended Highland whiskies, rum and wines. The last occupant of the inn was publican Robert Gentleman, who is seen here in the entrance way. In the 1950s road alignment works necessitated the demolition of the Inn and the surrounding properties. Included in these was Mary Bryce's little sweetie shop, which occupied part of the ground floor of the tenement adjacent to the inn. Today new housing occupies the Bridgehill site.

This photograph, looking east, shows the railway ticket office at Avonbridge. To the right of the station building (and to the extreme right of the photo) is Bogo View on Main Street. At one time this single-storey cottage contained Avonbridge Bakery and, following its removal from the Alberdt Buildings, the Avonbridge Post Office. In 1893 the bakery-cum-grocer shop was run by the Binnie family and, latterly, by the Smart family. In addition to bakery items (all of which were made in the bakery situated below the shop), groceries such as sugar, cheese and butter were also sold. During the Smart family's occupancy, particular favourites with local children were currant slices (or 'fly cemeteries'!) and bags of broken biscuits. The latter were either sold for a penny or exchanged for an empty glass lemonade bottle. Among the more unusual items sold from the bakery were tins of whitewash (used to paint the outside of the houses). Although initially a horse and cart was used for deliveries, by the 1950s the Smarts had three vans on the road. Today a modern bungalow called The Old Bakery stands on the site of the shop.

Avonbridge, viewed from the Whinny Braes. Some of the older properties on either side of Main Street to the north of the railway station buildings can be seen and these include Whinny Brae, the two-storey property whose white-washed gable end faces the camera. It still stands but to its right, on the Bogie Road, is part of the 'White Raw' which has since been demolished. Also demolished are the older properties on Main Street, between Avonbridge Parish Church (on the extreme left) and Whinny Brae. To the south of the railway station, and in the centre of the photograph, can be seen the rear of the Bridgehill properties while, to their right (and beyond the station), the long-roofed building with the white gable end was previously Gardner's woollen mill. This building was later used, variously, for plays put on by travelling theatre companies, as a picture house and, finally, as a haulage shed. Beyond this are Forrester's Buildings, Rosebank (with its distinctive twin roof dormers), and properties on Slamannan Road.

In this view, taken around 1910, can be seen some of the children from the 'White Raw'. These cottages were for the most part inhabited by mining families or employees of Waugh's Avonbridge Mill, and were quite basic by today's standards. For example, there were no inside toilets; instead families had to use a shed located at the foot of their garden. Access to the cottages was by means of a rutted farm track, known locally as the Bogie Road. This track ran eastwards, terminating south of the railway line at Bogo Farm. This farm (which included a steading) amounted to about 241 acres and in 1865 was occupied by James Kirkwood. Later, and until his retirement in 1902, it was one of three farms (the others being Bridgehill and Foggarmountain) owned by William Wilson, a member of Slamannan School Board. In 1922 a golf course was laid out at Bogo by Avonbridge & District Golf Club and a pavilion was added in 1928. In later years the club relocated to Bridgend.

In 1893, seemingly in response to a plea by Avonbridge co-operators, a branch of the Slamannan Co-operative Society was opened on Main Street, at Bridgehillend. This branch, known locally as the 'big' co-operative store, was a two-storey red and yellow brick building comprising a grocery with storage facilities above the shop. To access the storage area, incoming goods had to be winched up through a trapdoor – a procedure which proved to be extremely difficult as the winch did not have a brake. A single-storey extension attached to the store provided accommodation for the branch's salesman. Like other Slamannan Co-operative buildings, its interior was furbished with a wooden floor and a counter which extended along three sides. Although initially boots and drapery items had to be ordered specially from the Slamannan store, a separate drapery department was eventually opened nearby. In 1961, after the construction of new housing at the other end of the village, a second branch was opened in a wooden hut further down Main Street. However, both the hut and the Bridgehillend branch were eventually closed, to be replaced with a new purpose-built store.

Since 1804 there have been two churches which have occupied the prominent site at the junction of Main Street and Standburn Road. The first was an Associate Burgher Church built by Charles Shaw of Dalquhairn and Robert Waddell of Holehouse at a cost of £198. Completed in 1804, with the Rev. John Craig as its first minister, it was extended in 1815 when galleries were added, thereby increasing the seating capacity to 308. In 1820 it became a United Secession Church and in 1847 a United Presbyterian Church, before finally being demolished in 1889. The second church on the site was a Gothic-style building designed by the Falkirk-based architects A. & W. Black at a cost of £1,500, during the ministry of the Rev. John L. Robertson. Opened and dedicated by the Rev. John Smith of Edinburgh in February 1890, the new church could seat 200 people, with space for an additional sixty in the small gallery erected at the west end of the church. In addition, a modest church hall was built onto the east end of the church. Of the older properties seen here to left of the church, only the single-storey property nearest camera remains. This is Quarrybank Cottage, which dates from 1893. It was once the residence of the quarry master of the adjacent freestone quarry, which was owned by Henry Morrison, a slate merchant of Glasgow.

In August 1894 the 831-acre Gowanbank Estate to the south of Avonbridge, belonging to the late J.C. Rennie, was put up for sale for the upset price of £14,500. It was then described as a 'desirable residential estate with handsome and commodious mansion house and offices surrounded by beautiful policies and shrubberies containing many valuable plants'. Only two years before, a large number of golden yews, pyramidal English yews, golden, silver and green hollies, araucarias and rhododendrons, growing in the ornamental policies of Gowanbank had been sold by roup and had realised high prices. In 1913 the policies were further diminished with the sale of blown timber, consisting of 420 spruce, 430 Scots pine and sixty hardwood trees – the latter, it was stated, being very suitable for pit wood. Equally interesting was the collection of unique buildings erected on the estate by the architect Sir James Gowan. These include the Tower House, Bell House, Bath House, Tunnel House, Lodge House and Gingerbread House. In recent years all of these buildings have been renovated by developers.

Apart from a few substantial properties along its Main Street, the former mining village of Standburn largely comprised six long miners' rows. These rows which, in this 1900s photograph, are obscured by the tall Miners' Welfare Hall to the right of the photograph, at one time accommodated upwards of 1,000 people. In 1930 a report commissioned by Stirling County Council found them to be damp and overcrowded with inadequate sewerage and drainage, and with communal washing blocks. As a consequence, in the mid-1930s about 800 residents were resettled (often against their wishes) in a new model village on the Westquarter Estate, about five miles away. Ironically, this estate was bought from coal master James Nimmo, who owned most of the twelve local mines. In contrast to people's living conditions, the Miners' Welfare Institute was well-appointed and comprised a hall with several billiards tables and a well-stocked library and reading room upstairs. Built at a cost of £1,700, the institute was officially opened in 1900 by James Nimmo and later handed over to a board of trustees. The institute was eventually demolished in 1937.

By all accounts, the annual Drumbowie Public School Children's Gala was the highlight of the Standburn social calendar. Prior to Gala Day, the miners' wives would be busy sewing costumes for the historical pageant, while their husbands would be engaged in the construction of the wooden arches which were erected throughout the village. Window shutters and doors would also be painted and pavement kerbs whitened. Alongside each of the six miners rows, banners and bunting would be erected. Undoubtedly, however, the highlight of the day was the parade itself. By tradition, the band which was to head the parade would start playing upon their arrival at Bowhouse Station and continue to play throughout the duration of their one-mile walk from the station to the 'top of the gullet', where they would play especially loudly. The assembly point was within the school playground and thereafter the parade, led by a pupil on horseback, would make its way down Main Street and round the 'rows' before arriving at Fairview Park for refreshments and an afternoon of sports. Afterwards, many of the adults would make for Gothenburg public house, known locally as the 'squech', before later putting on their best 'togs' for the Gala Day dance held in the Miners' Welfare Hall.